Coping™

COPING WITH
RACIAL
PROFILING

Del Sandeen

Rosen
YA™

New York

Published in 2020 by The Rosen Publishing Group, Inc.
29 East 21st Street, New York, NY 10010

Library of Congress Cataloging-in-Publication Data

Names: Sandeen, Del, author.
Title: Coping with racial profiling / Del Sandeen.
Description: First edition. | New York : Rosen Publishing, 2020. | Series: Coping | Includes bibliographical references and index.
Identifiers: LCCN 2018049156| ISBN 9781508187400 (library bound) | ISBN 9781508187394 (pbk.)
Subjects: LCSH: Racial profiling in law enforcement—United States—Juvenile literature. | Discrimination in criminal justice administration—United States—Juvenile literature. | Racism—United States—Juvenile literature. | United States—Race relations—Juvenile literature.
Classification: LCC HV7936.R3 S26 2020 | DDC 363.2/308900973—dc23
LC record available at https://lccn.loc.gov/2018049156

Manufactured in China

For many of the images in this book, the people photographed are models. The depictions do not imply actual situations or events.

CONTENTS

INTRODUCTION

In December 2012, near Ferguson, Missouri, police officers pulled over an African American man named Arnold Cole. According to an article by Tony Messenger and Matt Sullivan in the *Guardian*, officers told Cole that his license plate bulb wasn't working. Cole was frustrated that such a minor issue led to the stop. He told the officers this. That's when they yelled at him to get out of his truck. Before Cole was able to open his door, one officer tried to yank it open. When he was unable to open it, the officer said he'd break the window with his baton.

Cole got out of his truck. The officer stood there with his gun aimed at Cole's chest, his finger on the trigger.

Cole put his hands up and his phone fell out of his pocket. He bent down to pick it up. One officer handcuffed him. They also called for a police dog, which searched the vehicle.

After a search, the officers found nothing.

However, the officers arrested Cole. They said he had not obeyed a lawful order. Cole was at the police station for twenty-four hours. He wasn't allowed to make any phone calls until the next morning.

Being pulled over by police is an all-too-common situation for many black and brown men across America. They're more likely to be subjected to racial profiling, harassment, and arrest.

After Cole was released, he hired a lawyer. Cole knew he hadn't done anything wrong.

His attorney asked to see the police dashcam video, which would have recorded the encounter, but the department refused. Cole's lawyer filed an appeal to have the charges dismissed. The police wouldn't back down from the tickets they gave him

Protests are nothing new in American society. In the wake of high-profile police shootings of unarmed African Americans, more people of all colors are making their voices heard.

for the window tint and the lightbulb. Cole contacted a local news station and newspaper. He was ready to contact the US Department of Justice as well as the American Civil Liberties Union (ACLU). The ACLU is a legal organization that works to protect and preserve Americans' rights. However, his lawyer

Michael Brown's mother, Lesley McSpadden, at a news conference in Jennings, Missouri, days after her son was fatally shot by a white police officer. The officer was not charged with a crime.

told him to wait before getting the government and the ACLU involved. After more than a year, Cole's case finally came to an end.

Many black men like Cole know how it feels to get pulled over for minor (sometimes nonexistent) offenses. To have to deal with police who harass and threaten them. When the police target people based solely on the color of their skin, that's racial profiling.

Cole knows that his story could have had a tragic ending. Less than two years later, in August 2014, a white police officer fatally shot Michael Brown in Ferguson.

It can be hard to find statistics on racial profiling. Numbers on racial profiling mainly come from investigations and research. Research supports that African Americans are more likely to be victims of racial profiling, especially black men. But Hispanics, Asians, and Native Americans are also subject to this type of discriminatory practice.

If you ever believe you've been racially profiled, you'll feel a lot of emotions. You might want to know what you can do about it. This book will show you how to cope with racial profiling. It will also show you how to react in positive, productive ways. If enough people come together to fight this injustice, racial profiling—and all the bad consequences of it—can finally come to an end.

CHAPTER ONE

When People Use Race to Judge

The world is made up of many races and ethnicities. Some nations are very homogenous. This means that most of their citizens share many physical characteristics—they look alike. Other countries, like the United States, have a rich history made up of different cultures. Unfortunately, not everyone appreciates such diversity. Some people make judgments about others without knowing them.

What happens when authority figures make race-based assumptions about certain groups of people? What happens when police think certain groups are more likely to be criminals? That's racial profiling.

What Is Racial Profiling?

Racial profiling is what happens when you assume things about someone based on that person's race, ethnicity, nation of origin, or religion. Profiling often occurs in the legal system. Some police officers take part in this type of discrimination.

The law doesn't always treat everyone equally. Although justice is supposed to be blind, meaning that everyone is judged the same, many people are not. According to 2016 Federal Bureau of Investigation (FBI) "Crime in the United States" statistics, black and brown people are arrested in disproportionate rates, or more often, compared to white people. They also get longer jail sentences than white people. This happens even when they commit the same crime. They might also have a similar criminal history. It's especially true for drug offenses.

In the 1990s, the Maryland State Police had to adopt a nondiscrimination policy. This was the result of a civil rights lawsuit. Before the lawsuit, state police sent out a report to officers. The report said that black people were bringing a lot of crack

When police officers stop minority drivers more than white drivers—even though drivers of all races commit offenses equally—this is a form of racial profiling.

cocaine into the state. The report listed several roads the drug traffickers were supposed to be using. Due to this, police focused more on black drivers driving on those roads, although in reality people of all races traveled those same streets. Officers thought that many of the people they stopped were criminals.

One of the things the lawsuit showed was that white and black drivers committed traffic violations equally, which Kenneth Meeks wrote about in *Driving*

While Black: Highways, Shopping Malls, Taxicabs, Sidewalks: How to Fight Back if You Are a Victim of Racial Profiling. What happened when the police did find drugs? Both white and black people had them in equal numbers. The police searched seven times more black drivers than they did white drivers. Because of this, it looked like African Americans

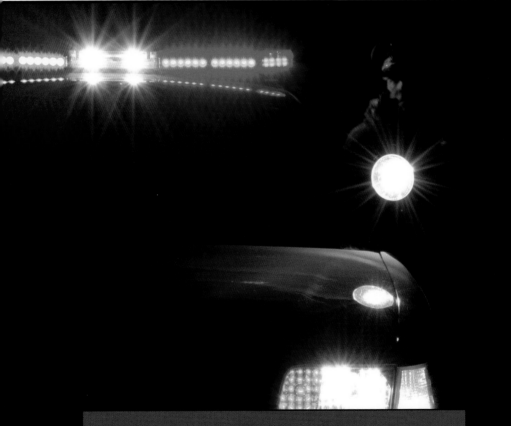

If you are ever pulled over by a police officer, how you react can make a big difference in the outcome. Try to remember to stay calm, especially if you've done nothing wrong.

were committing more crimes. But when police only focus on one group, they're more likely to find problems in that group.

Race Affects Everyone

Legal professionals aren't the only ones who racially profile people. School teachers and even the average person on the street may do it. They might judge a person only on the color of his skin or her country of origin. People of color have been racially profiled while shopping or traveling.

Immigration agents stop Hispanic travelers at bus stops across America on a regular basis. These agents ask travelers about their immigration status. Legally, agents can stop people who are within 100 miles (161 kilometers) of an international border. But the majority of Latinos in America are either born here or are naturalized citizens. A naturalized citizen is someone who legally becomes a citizen of a country. According to the Pew Research Center, only one-third of Latinos are immigrants. However, authority and nonauthority figures often single them out for questioning.

The ACLU states that "82 percent of foreign citizens stopped by Border Patrol in Michigan are Latino," according to an article by Niraj Warikoo in the *Detroit Free Press*. Foreign citizens are those who are not legal US citizens. It's not uncommon to see border patrol agents looking at travelers at bus stations. Sometimes, they question the travelers. But only a small number (2 percent) of foreign citizens who have been stopped in Michigan have any sort of criminal record, according to the ACLU.

The Trouble with Reasonable Doubt

Police officers can stop someone who they believe is taking part in—or even about to take part in—some type of criminal activity. This standard of reasonable suspicion is easy to meet. Cops don't need to actually see any evidence to stop a person. They can simply say that they have a reason to suspect the person may be involved in a crime. Many black and brown people are stopped while they're engaging in perfectly innocent activities. It may simply be due to where they are.

By meeting the low standards of reasonable suspicion, police can stop an African American man

This border station along the US-Mexico border is in Nogales, Arizona. There are nearly two thousand miles (3,219 kilometers) of border between the two countries, with six hundred of those miles separated by some sort of barrier.

who's running in an area with a higher than average crime rate. They can question him, even though he might only be running because he's in a hurry and not because he's fleeing a crime scene.

When officers focus more on blacks and Latinos, they have a higher chance of finding them breaking some sort of law. However, this doesn't mean that these groups commit more crimes. What it means is that when police target certain people and ignore others, it's only natural that they'll find problems in the group they focus on.

The law stands behind the concept of reasonable suspicion. Police officers and others in the criminal justice system must admit that racial profiling exists. They must also find ways to fix this type of discrimination. Until then, we will keep seeing the unfairness in the entire criminal process. Stops, arrests, and jail sentences affect black and brown people much more often and much more severely than they do white people.

Types of Racial Profiling

Race is usually the main factor in profiling. But it's not the only one. Religion is also a factor. This has become more common since the terrorist attacks of September 11, 2001. The group that said it was responsible for the attacks, al-Qaeda, was from Middle Eastern nations. Islam is the main religion in these countries.

Many people started to blame the religion instead of the individuals. They are practicing Islamophobia. This is a fear of Islam and Muslim people that results from negative stereotypes.

That's what happened with the January 2017 "Muslim Ban" in the United States. This executive order from President Donald Trump tried to stop people from coming to America if they were from seven specific countries. In these nations, Islam is the main religion. However, the ban isn't backed up by anything in the US Constitution. The ACLU and federal judges have worked against the ban or outright blocked it. New versions of the ban have been created. Muslim Ban 3.0 is a travel ban that doesn't allow most people from certain countries to come to America. These countries include Chad, Libya, Somalia, Iran, Syria, Venezuela, North Korea, and Yemen. US Supreme Court justice Sonia Sotomayor criticized the judges who voted to uphold the ban, and she blamed hostility toward Islam as motivating it.

Most Muslim women wear the traditional head covering, called a hijab. What happens when they

Many Americans protested President Trump's orders banning people from certain countries from entering the United States. Protesters felt the ban was racially motivated.

get targeted at airports for extra screenings? This is racial profiling. It also profiles their religion. They may be students, business professionals, and American citizens. But their clothing can make them a target. It can be worse when anti-Islamic feelings are at an all-time high.

Sikhs, as well, may feel they face extra scrutiny. Sikh men typically wear turbans. Sikh women

Many Muslim women wear a hijab, a traditional head covering, in public. This can cause others to make unfair assumptions about their beliefs without getting to know them.

wear long scarves on their heads. Someone who is unfamiliar with the Sikh faith may believe that Sikh is a nationality, but it is a religion. Most people who practice Sikhism are from the northern Indian state of Punjab.

Again, it's important not to make assumptions. If you don't know anything about someone, educate yourself. Everyone can learn about different cultures, peoples, and religions to understand more about them.

Who Takes Part in Racial Profiling?

Anyone can profile another person based on race. Someone might know that making assumptions based on skin color or nation of origin is wrong. But people sometimes do it anyway.

Is it unconscious bias that causes someone to call the police when she sees an unfamiliar person of color walking or driving in her neighborhood? There has been more publicity in recent years over white citizens calling the police on minorities who aren't doing anything illegal, thanks in part to social media.

White people have called police to report black people barbequing in a public park. They've also called to report young black teens selling bottled water on the sidewalk. Callers never name race as a reason for the phone calls. But, many of these calls single out black and brown people. Is profiling—and racism—the real reason?

When a retail store worker targets black and brown people as potential shoplifters much more often than he does white shoppers, he's racially profiling.

Consider the April 2018 incident that happened in a Philadelphia, Pennsylvania, Starbucks. According to a *Washington Post* article by Rachel Siegel, two African American men, Rashon Nelson and Donte Robinson, were waiting for a friend to meet them at the coffee spot. One of them asked to use the restroom. Starbucks employees wouldn't let them because the men hadn't bought anything. They were told that restrooms were only for paying customers. Nelson and Robinson said they were waiting on a friend for a business meeting.

They continued to wait. When an employee asked if they needed anything, they said no and that they were fine.

That's when store employees asked them to leave. The men refused to do so because they were still waiting. The store manager then called 911. The manager told the operator that the two men wouldn't buy anything or leave.

Crime Statistics versus "Shopping While Black"

"Driving while black" is a well-known problem caused by racial profiling in black communities. So is "shopping while black." Black customers get followed around more in stores. Store workers say it's to stop shoplifting. But black shoppers also wait longer in customer service lines. These forms of profiling are subtle. They're not easy to prove.

Workers sometimes blame someone's clothing for the profiling. They may say they made judgments because a person wore baggy pants or worn-out sneakers. However, it's been shown that clothing isn't necessarily the issue. Even when black and white shoppers wear similar clothes, store workers still watch the black shoppers more closely. Workers also follow them more often. Many African Americans know how this feels.

Some people claim that black people commit the most crimes in the United States. According to FBI statistics, in 2016, white people were arrested for committing almost 70 percent of all crimes. Black people were arrested for nearly 27 percent. A look at the numbers clearly shows that African Americans do not commit the most amount of crimes in this country.

Police officers showed up. They arrested the men without incident, meaning that they caused no trouble. Witnesses in Starbucks filmed the arrest on their phones. They also told the officers that the two men had done nothing wrong. The video shows that the two were calm as police handcuffed them.

Their friend, Andrew Yaffe, came in at that point and wanted to know why they were being arrested. The young white man questioned the officers. He told them that they'd been waiting for him to show up.

The arrest video went viral on social media. This led to bad publicity for Starbucks. The manager who called the police left the company. The two charges the men were arrested on—trespassing and creating a disturbance—were dropped.

It wasn't the first or only time customers accused Starbucks employees of racially profiling them. In Los Angeles, California, Brandon Ward, an African American man, asked to use the restroom before he bought anything. Store employees refused to give him the restroom code. They said the restroom was only for paying customers. However, he noticed a white man walking out of the restroom. Ward asked him if he'd bought anything before the employees gave him the code. The white man said, "No."

Ward captured this conversation on his phone. He shared it on social media.

At first, someone may find it hard to say that race had anything to do what happened to Nelson, Robinson, and Ward. However, racial profiling comes into play when you look at the facts. White people are able to sit and wait or get the restroom code without having to buy anything first. Is it store policy that everyone has to buy something first? If so, the policy should apply to everyone. But it doesn't always seem to.

Racial Profiling in Our Communities

For the past two decades, violent crimes have decreased, according to a sourcebook of criminal justice statistics. But the level of trust people have in the police has not risen. It's important to look at how racial profiling affects the way people view police officers.

A Long and Troubling History

Racial profiling isn't new. There may be more publicity about it now, but this kind of discrimination has been around for a long time in America.

The 1855 California Vagrancy Act targeted Latinos. This act was commonly known as the

Greaser Act. The term "greaser" is derogatory and racist. The act was supposed to focus on vagrants. But, it really focused on Spanish-speaking people. According to the act, people who were "armed and not peaceable and quiet persons" were the problem, as stated in an article by Lupe S. Salinas and Fernando Colon-Navarro at Racism.org. Authorities were allowed to target vagrants under this act. But they really used the act to oppress Latinos—particularly those of Mexican descent. Whites used acts like these to make life harder for many people of color.

Statistics from a 1996 report by Marianne O. Nielsen and Robert A. Silverman titled "American Indians in Prison" show how poorly Native Americans fare in the justice system as well. According to the report, in South Dakota, Native Americans make up about 7 percent of the population. However, they make up about 26 percent of all prisoners in the state penitentiary. These disproportionate numbers are similar in other states, such as Idaho, North Dakota, Oklahoma, Oregon, and Minnesota.

While police officers kill more white people overall, officers kill blacks at disproportionate

Today, Native American people make up just 1 percent of the US population. The group pictured here is part of the Spirit Lake Reservation.

rates to whites. According to a 2015 article in *The Guardian* by Jon Swaine, Oliver Laughland, and Jamiles Lartey, unarmed "black Americans are more than twice as likely" to be killed by police compared to white Americans.

does if they believe it works. So when the DEA says it doesn't racially profile but then targets minorities, the message contradicts itself.

The Relationship Between Cops and Communities

About half of all Americans trust cops. But when you look at how many black people trust the police, that number is very different. African Americans are about "20–30 percent less likely" to trust cops than whites, according to *Policing the Black Man: Arrest, Prosecution, and Imprisonment* by Angela J. Davis. These numbers are important because blacks are more often the victims in violent crimes. Why, then, don't they have more trust as the level of violent crimes has fallen?

Black people may trust the police less because of how they're treated in their own neighborhoods. For example, a lot of cops might patrol areas that have a high minority population. Are the cops keeping the people safe? Or are they harassing them?

Imagine how that must feel. You live in an area where there's a lot of police officers. But they don't

Your experiences shape your perceptions. Sometimes white people, who have only had harassment-free interactions with the police, are surprised to hear about bad cop behavior.

make you feel safe. Instead, they're constantly bothering you, even when you're not doing anything wrong. When people don't think the police treat them fairly, it's hard for them to trust them.

This is evident when you look at how white youth and black youth view cops. The more contact teens have with police, the more likely it is they'll have conflict. Because black teens have more interactions with the police than white teens, blacks tend to have more negative attitudes toward cops. White teens consider bad police actions to be rare. But black teens see police misconduct as the norm.

Young people in predominantly black communities often feel like the police stop them constantly. It happens when they're walking down the

Black and brown drivers can feel they're targeted just because of the color of their skin. They may believe this if they're stopped frequently for minor offenses, like not using a turn signal.

street. It happens when they're driving on the road. In St. Louis, Missouri, young black boys complained about the constant harassment, according to Davis's *Policing the Black Man.* They said they could be stopped five or six times in one day. Officers stopped them to pat them down and ask them questions.

It's not only St. Louis where things like this happen. In Washington, DC, young black boys get the same harassment. It's worse when they already have a police record. Teens report that the same officers continue to harass them. As detailed in *Policing the Black Man* by Davis, in one instance, twin brothers were arrested four times in a few weeks. The officers who arrested them were the same every time. Arrests were for minor offenses. It was clear to the court that these officers had a grudge against the twins. So, prosecutors stopped charging over these petty crimes.

Stop and Frisk

Stop and frisk is a police policy that means that when police believe they have a good reason to stop someone, they can detain them temporarily. During this time, the police can pat the person down. They might believe the person has a weapon or drugs.

During the 1990s, however, it became clear that New York City cops were using this policy unfairly and aggressively. Police officers were only supposed to pat down someone if they thought they were in danger. They had to believe the person might have a weapon on him. A cop could say he saw a bulge under the person's shirt that he thought was a gun.

However, police were stopping people and frisking them even when they weren't worried about their safety. In many cases, there was no reason for the officers to think a person had a gun or other weapon. Reasonable suspicion isn't the same as having a hunch. Police officers can only form suspicions if a person is acting in a suspicious way.

Here's an example: A man is walking down the street. He sees a police car parked at the curb ahead of him. He stops and then turns around to go back the way he came. Police might suspect he's doing something wrong because he makes an effort to avoid them.

Tough on Crime versus Community Outreach

Is a tough on crime policy better than community outreach? It depends on the results you want.

New York City underwent a drastic change in the 1990s. Before then, the city had a bad reputation for its level of crime. Rudolph Giuliani was elected mayor around this time. He adopted a zero-tolerance policy. This included no tolerance for even minor offenses. There was heavy police presence. There was also a lot of stop and frisk occurring.

While this reduced crime rates, it didn't build up trust in the police force. Many minorities have felt victimized by the stop and frisk program that was heavily used during this time.

Now, consider how San Diego, California, handled crime during this same period. The Chief of Police at the San Diego Police Department took a different approach. Jerry Sanders decided to use community efforts as one way to fight crime. His department focused more on building

(continued on the next page)

(continued from the previous page)

relationships between officers and citizens. About 1,200 people in the community joined a group that worked with the police. Together, they found ways to prevent and fight crime.

Crime dropped in San Diego during this time. What surprised some is that crime levels dropped even more there than in New York City, even though San Diego didn't have as many police officers. All types of crime were reduced, including murder.

One of the biggest differences between the two cities is the relationship between the police and the citizens. In New York, tension continues between the two. But in San Diego, there's a feeling of cooperation.

But just walking down the street, even in a neighborhood that has a lot of crime, isn't a good enough reason to stop someone and frisk them.

The stop and frisk policy has been shown to be a major cause of "friction between the police and minority groups," according to *Profiles in Injustice* by David A. Harris. Minorities often feel they're targeted for stop and frisk more than whites. Black and brown people believe they're stopped unfairly. This leads to tension between police and citizens.

Racial profiling is one of the causes of so many arrests in minority communities. "Cops stop and search black men at higher rates than" whites, according to *Policing the Black Man* by Angela J. Davis. Unfortunately, it's legal for police to do so.

What Happens When There's No Trust?

When you don't trust someone, do you try and talk to them? Do you tell them important things going on in your life? Would you tell them a secret? Probably not.

When black and brown people don't trust police officers, they're less likely to report things to them. This is what happens with the no-snitching policy that some minorities use. Even when they know who did something wrong, they won't tell the

When police shot and killed an unarmed homeless man in Los Angeles, LAPD officers attended a town hall meeting. There activists and residents vented and demanded answers.

police. They consider it snitching. It can be hard for someone living in an area once his neighbors know that he talks to the police. They might not trust him the same way that they don't trust cops.

When does this lack of trust begin? Most people form their opinions of police and the justice system when they're teenagers. Black and brown teens who have a lot of conflicts with police officers are affected by that as they grow up. The problem doesn't just affect how kids view cops. According to Davis's *Policing the Black Man*, it becomes a problem for "public safety, officer safety" and the lives of boys and men in minority communities.

It's an issue of public safety when people know who did something wrong but won't tell the authorities. Someone who's done something violent—including murder—is able to walk around free because no one wants to turn him in. It's an issue of officer safety because police have one more criminal on the streets to deal with.

Myths & FACTS

Myth: Black people steal more often than white people.

Fact: According to FBI statistics for 2016, 69 percent of people charged with larceny-theft were white, while 27 percent were black. Unfortunately, because of the stereotype that blacks steal more than whites, retailers often focus on black shoppers. This is a form of racial profiling better known as retail discrimination. It's one that many black customers have experienced in subtle and direct ways.

Myth: Undocumented Latino immigrants are taking over American jobs.

Fact: Of the Latino people in the US workforce, only 5 percent are undocumented immigrants, according to the Pew Research Center. Construction and farming are the only businesses that have a higher than average number of Hispanic workers. All other businesses have mostly US-born employees. These employees may be white, black, Asian, Native American, or Hispanic, born in America.

Myth: The religion of Islam promotes terrorism.

Fact: Islam, like other major world religions, has a basis of peace. In fact, the word "Islam" stems from the Arabic word "salam," which means "peace." Muslims greet other Muslims by wishing them peace. The term "jihad" doesn't tell Muslims to commit violence for their religion. It only directs them to a deeper understanding of Islam and, if necessary, to defend it. Unfortunately, a small number of Muslims have misused the religion of Islam for their actions. But no major religion promotes violence or hatred.

CHAPTER THREE

Biases and Division

No one is born racist. A person may be born into a racist family. His parents may teach hateful stereotypes. But hating others based on skin color or ethnicity is something that we learn.

How and Why People Form Biases

Parents teach their children lots of things. Some of them are good, such as how to share or ride a bike. Some of them are not good, such as judging people based on race, ethnicity, or religion. According to an article in the *Boston Globe* by James H. Burnett III, Harvard University psychologist Mahzarin Banaji reports that when parents say racist things in front of their children, kids accept that racism.

Children might also pick up racist beliefs from other people in their family. As a result, they may choose friends who hold those same views. It's common to want to be around people who think like you. For younger people, especially, being with like-minded people makes you feel a part of something.

Before people learn racism, however, they learn race awareness. Researchers have found that children as young as three are very aware of racial differences. Most children are also familiar with racism.

However, in books on childhood development, there's often no mention of these types of issues. Adults who work with children, such as teachers, social workers, and child psychologists, may not realize how aware children are of race. These adults may use books that don't talk about children and racism in their training to work with kids. They might then believe that children don't see color when it comes to skin.

Other adults, too, may think that they shouldn't talk to kids about these differences. They believe children won't be prejudiced if they avoid the topic. Some adults don't think they should talk about the

You can learn a lot by talking to those from other races and religions. Going to a school with a diverse population can help students form their own opinions about other cultures.

physical and cultural differences between people. They might believe they can deny racism exists if they avoid talking about it. But the issue they're avoiding is very serious.

Other ways someone may develop biased viewpoints could stem from the stories and images she hears and sees via the media. For example, consider a white woman who lives in an all-white community. She has little to no contact with black people in real life. How does she form her opinions about black people? What happens if she forms them only based on what she sees on television?

This is a problem because African Americans don't commit most of the crimes in the United States, according to 2016 numbers provided by the FBI. But, news programs and crime-based reality shows may show blacks being arrested and led away in handcuffs more often than whites. When someone mostly sees images like this, she might believe that black people commit more crimes than people of other races. She may form prejudices against anyone with black or brown skin. This is emotionally harmful to her. It also doesn't give her the chance to connect with those who look different from her.

The Effects of Prejudice

If a person acts on his biases, he may harm people he is prejudiced against. When someone commits a violent act motivated by prejudice, that's a hate crime. But prejudice can also hurt the person holding those biased views.

"I'm Not Racist!"

Not all racism is conscious. When some people say that they're not racist, they may really believe that they're not. What they might not realize is that they hold inherent biases against people of other ethnicities or cultures. This means they have prejudiced beliefs that they don't really think about. Instead, they believe things about other people without giving much thought to why they have those beliefs.

Unconscious racism is what happens when you instantly think of a young black or Latino man when you hear the word "criminal." If you automatically associate terms like "thug" with African Americans or "illegals" with Hispanics—that's unconscious racism. It's not always easy to recognize when you do this, because many people hold stereotypes about other races.

Stereotypes, even the seemingly positive ones, are harmful. They promote blanket beliefs about other people that are often false. When you stereotype others, you don't consider the individuals. You only consider the whole culture or race.

Missing Out

What happens when you don't take the time to get to know someone? What if you form opinions based on what your parents and friends say? Do you believe biased perspectives you see in the media? Then you don't give yourself the chance to really find out what people in other groups are like. This limits your view of the world.

Some white people live in a bubble of white-centeredness. Most of the people they see and deal with on a daily basis are white. To their minds, this is their entire world. But this isn't anything like reality. Children who grow up in white-centered worlds are "robbed of opportunities for emotional and intellectual growth," according to Judy Katz in her handbook, *White Awareness: Handbook for Anti-Racism Training*. This stunts them emotionally and intellectually. It lowers their chances of appreciating anything that's different from what they're used to.

Job Hunting Made Harder

For the people who are the victims of discrimination, life is often more difficult. Not only does racism

When people don't take the time to make friends with those who are different from them, they can miss out on valuable friendships and learning opportunities. Shutting people out is harmful to all.

affect them in school, it can also have an effect on the jobs they get in life. A study published by the *Harvard Business Review* in 2017 showed that white job applicants received more callbacks than black and Latino applicants. According to the study, even when the applicants had the same résumé, whites were called back 36 percent more often than blacks and 24 percent more often than Latinos.

Unfair Sentencing

If minorities are involved in any type of criminal activity, they usually suffer longer-lasting, more detrimental effects than white people in the same situation. In a report published by the US Sentencing Commission in 2012, black men received longer sentences than white men for the same crimes, averaging 19 percent longer. The news is worse in certain states. For prisoners serving life sentences, blacks make up 60 percent of this group overall. In Georgia and Louisiana, blacks make up more than 73 percent in each state, according to a 2014 ACLU report on racial disparities in sentencing.

Making Assumptions

Racism also makes people from different communities not trust those from other communities.

Journalist Ellis Cose wrote a book called *The Rage of a Privileged Class*. As he puts it in the book by Kenneth Meeks, *Driving While Black*, "people generally

Racial profiling by attorneys and judges in courtrooms can lead to stiffer sentences for people of color. This also contributes to the disproportionate number of miniority prisoners in America.

assume all whites are middle class until they prove themselves different, while blacks and Latinos are generally assumed not to be middle class until they prove it." These types of assumptions are harmful and stand in the way of forming real connections with people who don't look like you.

Consider a man who lives a sheltered life. He's grown up in a white-centered place. He doesn't see different groups of people in his neighborhood or at work. What if he looks at black people with suspicion because he doesn't know any? Whenever he sees a black person walking in his neighborhood, he may think of code words and phrases such as "thug," "up to no good," or "he looks suspicious." The white man might call the police due to his suspicions, even if the black person is doing nothing wrong.

How to Counter Bias

Racism is learned behavior, which means you can stop holding racist views. It may not happen right away. You'll have to work at it. This may be harder to do if you're surrounded by friends and family who openly embrace racism.

Also, it can be difficult to let go of stereotypes and prejudices. Even when you know racism is wrong, it's tough to stop biased ways of thinking. However, that doesn't mean you should give up and think you can't make a difference just because you're one person.

Speak Up!

If you believe that someone has racially profiled you or you see an instance of profiling, speak up. Do not stay silent about it. Depending on the situation, you might not be able to say anything right away. As soon as it is safe to do so, however, you should let someone else know about it. It could be a parent, school administrator, or a teacher. Telling other people is one of the ways you can fight this type of discrimination.

People who do racist things count on not being exposed. That's why it's so important to speak up. By letting others know that this problem—racism—exists, you're also letting them know that it's not right.

Real People, Real Stories

Although statistics are clear numbers, real people are behind those numbers. Their stories are real, too. Here are some actual experiences of people from different ethnic groups.

College Tour Gone Wrong

In the spring of 2018, Thomas Kanewakeron Gray and Lloyd Skanahwati Gray traveled to Colorado State University. They had saved up their money and driven seven hours from their home in New Mexico to tour the university. The two showed up late, but when they arrived they joined the tour, already in progress.

According to an article in the *Rio Grande Sun* by Austin Fisher, a parent in the tour group called the police because she said the brothers made her nervous. She said they were acting strangely and that "they don't belong" on the tour. When police showed up, they talked to the brothers. They said they were quiet because one of the young men is shy. By the time the police were done with their questioning, the tour had moved on.

The college president put out a statement criticizing the incident. The school apologized to the brothers, who had initially viewed the college as their dream school. They went to a lot of trouble to visit the college. Their tour could have been more

Learning environments like colleges are often ideal places to meet people from different ethnic backgrounds and to expand your group of friends. You can learn about new cultures!

pleasant for them if they hadn't been pulled aside for questioning.

The reason that the parent gave for calling the police is debatable. She claimed the brothers weren't part of the tour. But they were. Her assumptions about them led to an incident that didn't have to happen.

Since then, the Gray family is working with the ACLU on a plan with the school. University officials have promised to make changes to their tour policy as well.

Unfair Airport Delays

Author of *The Headscarf Controversy: Secularism and Freedom of Religion*, Hilal Elver says that "the global terror network created racial profiling against Muslims," according to a *New York Times* article by Michael T. Luongo.

In the same article, lawyer, writer, and Muslim-American Nafees Syed says that she has to arrive at airports an hour earlier than anyone else, because she expects to be singled out for screening. She wears the traditional hijab. As a result, she gets pulled over "more often than not" at security check-ins for extra screenings and pat downs.

It's not only the clothing that calls attention to Muslim travelers. It's also their names. They may feel the stigma while traveling due to their religion.

Syed even avoids going through security with her peers who aren't Muslim. She says she doesn't

These Muslim women could be subjected to extra screenings in a US airport. Being pulled aside for additional pat-downs and searches can be inconvenient and humiliating.

"want them to see the humiliation" she's going to experience.

Transportation Security Administration (TSA) officials claim that they don't focus on specific religious groups. Instead, they blame extra scrutiny on getting clearer images under certain types of clothing. However, many Muslim Americans feel targeted as a result of the additional screenings they're often subject to.

Bad Baggy Clothes?

Two high-school honor students, Minhtran Tran and Quyen Pham, were using a pay phone outside of a mall in Garden Grove, California. Police confronted them and asked if they were in a gang. Officers said the girls were wearing gang clothing. What did this clothing look like? It was similar to what many other teens wear: baggy pants and fitted shirts.

The police didn't ask the girls or their parents for permission to take their pictures. Officers took Polaroid photos of the girls and asked them for information to identify themselves. Later on, the girls found out that officers had posted their photos on a bulletin board at the police station. Why would their pictures be posted at the station? They were not criminals.

Police had racially profiled the girls as part of their efforts to find Asian gang members. The officers believed the girls' clothing matched descriptions of how female gang members dressed. But, if the girls had worn something different, police could have targeted them anyway for being gang members "in disguise," according to a report profiling gang members as outlined in *Profiles in Injustice: Why Racial Profiling Cannot Work* by David A. Harris.

Horrible Hecklers

Los Angeles-born journalist Nick Valencia went to a musical festival in Atlanta, Georgia. There, he was speaking in Spanish to a group of people that was visiting from Mexico City. According to an article at Racism.org by Lupe S. Salinas and Fernando Colon-Navarro, a white person who heard the conversation told Valencia to "go home." This person clearly and wrongly assumed his home was not America. As he says, "to some, the brown color of my skin means I'm not...American." It doesn't matter if Latinos are born in America, are naturalized citizens, or undocumented. The anti-immigration policies sweeping across the country are taking their toll on them.

The Toll That Racial Profiling Takes

People who deal with racism and discrimination suffer more physical and mental health issues than

In 2018, a controversial policy to separate parents and children along the US-Mexico border was enacted, leading to public outcry and many protests across the United States.

people who don't. They're more stressed. Stress is a major factor in having a lower quality of life. Increased stress levels can lead to heart disease, body aches, and depressed moods.

With each story of injustice that we hear, we may feel anguish, frustration, and anger. Negative emotions like this can also result in poor health. People who feel the sting of discrimination have more incidents of heart and kidney disease.

Studying Prejudice

People are working to research racial profiling by police officers. Consider this study of a police training session conducted by Tom Hayes and Didi Nelson, as detailed in *Profiles in Injustice: Why Racial Profiling Cannot Work* by David A. Harris. Both Hayes and Nelson work in law enforcement. The two asked the class of police officers several race-based questions. The answers may be shocking.

Hayes asked, "What comes to your mind when I ask you to envision the face of crime? What do you think is the typical image of a criminal?"

After a few moments of uncomfortable silence, one of the officers spoke up: "Young black male."

Nelson then commented: "Isn't that what we see all the time on TV?"

Next, Hayes asked the officers what they would think if they saw a white teenager driving a new BMW. They replied their first thoughts would be that the kid is a "brat" or has "rich parents." When asked for their first thoughts if they saw a black teen driving the same car, the officers' answers are revealing. They admitted they'd think the car was stolen or that the driver was a drug dealer.

These are examples of racial profiling. Without knowing anything about the drivers, these officers admit to making assumptions. Just saying the words "crime" and "criminal" bring to mind a black face, with no other facts present.

Beliefs like this feed into the lack of trust that exists between law enforcement agencies and many in the black community.

Someone who racially profiles others may deny doing it. He might blame things like a person's clothing for profiling them. What is undeniable is the negative impact these incidents have. They affect individuals and entire communities.

What Are the Statistical Results of Racial Profiling?

African American boys go to juvenile detention more often than boys in other racial groups. According to the US Justice Department, more than 50 percent of the students who are arrested in US schools and referred to the juvenile justice system are black or Hispanic. Blacks and Latinos are disciplined more harshly than their white counterparts. Zero-tolerance policies that many schools have leave little to no room for even the most minor offenses. This may include bringing nail clippers to school.

When children enter the juvenile justice system, they're less likely to stay in school. They might not graduate high school or go to college. Instead, they may enter what is known as the school-to-prison pipeline. This is a situation where kids are pushed out of school and straight into the criminal justice system. When people don't have the educational background to secure a job, they tend to get into trouble with the law. Once kids are pushed out of the educational system, it's hard for them to get back in. Without this type of structure, too many of them turn to criminal activity because they don't believe they have any other options.

Why Words Matter

Consider the words that probation officers in the juvenile justice system use to describe kids.

When police officers engage with the community instead of only showing up when there's trouble, they can build a spirit of cooperation. This officer is talking about school safety.

Officers may say that white juveniles have environmental problems but describe black juveniles as having antisocial personalities.

Why does this matter? When counselors and other trained professionals work with kids in the system, they note such descriptions. They might treat a boy one way if they think he's only having peer pressure or family problems. But, if they believe a boy is dangerous, they'll treat him another way. As a result, black boys who are described with such negative terms are more likely to go into a juvenile detention center. White boys who aren't described so negatively may simply receive counseling while living at home.

Those facing discrimination can experience negative physical and mental effects. This can lead to shorter life expectancy and higher rates of certain medical conditions.

believe they'll suffer discrimination. This can lead to them missing out on important opportunities.

Celebration Gone Wrong

Roberto Montenegro's story is just one example of how a discriminatory experience can lead to negative effects, mentally and physically. In an article originally published in the *Journal of the American Medical Association* in 2016, he tells how he and his wife went out to dinner to celebrate him getting his PhD. After dinner, they left the restaurant. They were in line to get their car from one of the valets, who park and retrieve cars for customers. The valets wore red vests. Montenegro wore a suit.

Although he wasn't dressed like a valet, a woman pulled up in her car and handed her keys to him. Why did she assume he was one of the restaurant's valets? When Montenegro looked at them, he saw they looked Latino, like him. However, he wasn't dressed like them at all. He was too shocked to say anything to the woman. But, he said his heart began pounding. He felt confused, angry, and hurt.

That wasn't the end of it. A few minutes later, as he was still standing in line waiting for his car, another person gave him their keys. He should have been feeling happy and excited for his accomplishment. Instead, he said he felt "invisible," according to the article.

This night wasn't the first time Montenegro had experienced such racist assumptions. He, like other people of color, can be mistaken for anything from waiters to hospital aides instead of physicians. He's one of a growing number of scientists who are trying to figure out how constant experiences of racism affect a person's body. There are real health disparities across ethnic groups. Discrimination may have something to do with it.

Health Consequences

In a poll conducted by the Robert Wood Johnson Foundation and the Harvard T.H. Chan School of Public Health, researchers found that about one-third of Latinos report they've faced discrimination. They report all sorts of discriminatory actions. They have faced racism when they applied for jobs. They dealt with it when trying to find a place to live. They feel they don't earn the same money for doing the same job. They also hear racial slurs and other offensive comments. One researcher at the University of California, Berkeley, Amani Nuru-Jeter, is trying to answer the question of how racial experiences become differences in health. These differences include higher levels of heart disease and diabetes. It also includes higher rates of infant deaths.

Asian Discrimination Happens Too

Research shows that "discrimination is associated with poorer mental and physical health," according to an article in the US National Library of Medicine. Many Asians say they have experienced discrimination. But there has been very little research on how racism has affected them.

In a 2008 National Latino and Asian American Study, researchers looked at the connection between discrimination and mental health. More than 2,000 Asian Americans took part in the study. Some were born in the United States. Others were immigrants from different Asian countries.

The study examined different factors in how Asians reacted to racism against them. One of the factors was how strongly a person identified with his or her culture. On one hand, people who have a strong ethnic identity tend to suffer less distress when facing discrimination. On the other hand, these people recount more incidents of discrimination.

(continued on the next page)

(continued from the previous page)

Asian men report more discrimination than Asian women. But women report more mental health issues from dealing with discrimination.

One thing the study made clear is that the more discrimination someone faces, the more distress he or she feels. Additional research can lead to developing helpful resources. These resources can help people protect themselves against the negative effects of discrimination.

Positive Ways to Cope with Racial Profiling

Sometimes, people react to negative events with more negativity. This can harm them. Even if they don't suffer physically, they can suffer emotionally. Although bad things happen, you don't have to react in a negative way. You can take your anger or frustration and turn it into something positive. Try different things to make you feel better about any discrimination or racial profiling you experience.

By getting to know people from different backgrounds and countries, you may discover that you have more similarities than differences. Consider taking a genuine interest in others.

Be Creative

Use your creativity. Everyone can be creative. Maybe you don't draw or paint. So you don't think you're artistic. However, there are probably other creative things you can do.

If you like music, write songs about your experience. You can put all of your sad feelings into music. You can either write the song's lyrics or you can write the music. Play it yourself if you play any instruments. You can also partner with someone else and let them perform your piece.

Maybe you'd rather write your experiences down. You can put them in your personal journal. No one has to read them if you don't want them to. Just writing down what happened and how you feel about it is a creative outlet that can help you.

If you don't want to journal about it, write poems or stories. This can be helpful if you really wish your experience had a different outcome. When you create a story about it, you can write down the ending you want instead of what actually happened.

Talk It Out

Sometimes, it's hard to talk about bad things that happen to us. Holding onto those feelings can make you feel worse. Find someone you can talk to about how you feel. This may be a parent, teacher, other family member, or friends. The more support you have, the better you'll feel. Even if no one has a solution, just talking about hard things can make you feel better. You won't feel so alone when you see that other people have gone through the same things. This helps you feel less isolated.

Talking to a counselor is another option. It may be difficult to talk to someone you know. Talking to a therapist lets you talk about your problems but to someone who isn't biased for or against you. It could be a counselor at school. Or it could be someone outside of school.

Social Media in Small Doses

Social media has its good and bad points. When a police shooting makes national news, people might see it all over their social media timelines. Sometimes, hearing a lot of negative news stories can make people feel depressed. They might also see some people's reactions that make them angry. If being on social media makes you feel worse, step away from it. How long you choose not to be on Twitter, Snapchat, or Instagram is up to you. But feel free to take a break from something that makes you feel bad.

While social media can make connecting with others simple and quick, it also has its downsides. There's nothing wrong with taking a social media break and hanging out face to face.

Self-Care

You might have heard about self-care, but not be sure what it is. It simply means to take care of yourself. This doesn't only mean physically. It means mentally and emotionally, too. Sometimes, all of the negative things you see and hear can feel overwhelming. It's important to protect yourself from all of that negativity.

Different people find ways to practice self-care. Find a way that works for you. You could meditate or pray. Not everyone is religious, but you can still be spiritual. You don't have to pray to anyone in particular if you're not comfortable with that. A lot of people can find peace just by thinking of their place in the universe. If you find comfort by going to church, temple, or mosque, then continue to do that.

Another thing you can do is stay active. If you play sports, keep doing that. It doesn't matter if you play on a school team or you like jogging by yourself. Regular physical activity helps to lower stress levels. People who face discrimination are often under stress, and exercise to help reduce it. Exercise is shown to reduce anxiety, depression, and a negative mood. It also improves self-esteem and makes people more social.

Fight Against Injustice

Joining the fight against injustice and racism is another way to be socially active. Knowing you're doing something to combat a serious problem can empower you. It shows you how big a difference one person can make when you join with others.

Mexican folk dancers showcase a special aspect of their culture. The clothing, music, and dance style reflect the uniqueness of their history and customs.

Everyone should feel proud of who they are. If someone has discriminated against your culture, you might feel embarrassed about it. Remember, though, that America is a nation of immigrants. It's diversity that makes it different from other nations. Don't feel embarrassed about your culture. Celebrate it. Each person's ethnicity is unique and adds to the richness of American culture. You might still face discrimination. But when you're proud of who you are, you'll realize that if someone is biased against you, it has nothing to do with you. They're the ones with the problem.

Facing and Fighting Injustice

Fighting racism and unfairness isn't the job of one group. Everyone should take part in fighting against injustice. Even if you've never experienced racial profiling, you should take a stand against it whenever possible. When people work together for a cause, it brings them together. One of the best ways to put an end to racism and all of its negative effects is to cooperate with others who share the same goal.

Can You Recognize Racism and Racial Profiling?

Recognizing racism isn't always easy. Some people who discriminate against others do it in subtle ways. They're not as direct in their actions, so it's not always clear that racism is the cause of certain actions.

Accept that some people are never going to admit to their racism. They may act in discriminatory ways, but they'll use other reasons to explain why they did something. It will never be because they're biased.

They might say someone didn't get the job because another applicant was better qualified. A cab driver may pass by one person and pick up a group of white people on the next corner. A clerk may say he followed an individual around a store because he or she walked in with a large bag. Or, a clerk may give another reason, like the one in the following story.

Charles Ogletree, a professor at the Harvard School of Law, related an incident involving an African American artist. The artist went shopping in a department store. He bought a large amount of clothing that cost a couple of thousand dollars. He paid for his items with his credit card. After that, he left the store.

That was when a store clerk called the police. Officers arrived as the artist was getting into his car.

They arrested him and took him back inside the store. The police looked at his credit card receipt and his credit card. They discovered that he was the actual owner of the card.

Word got out about the incident. The following day, a news reporter asked the store clerk why she'd called the police on the artist. She claimed that race had nothing to do with it. She said she'd called because "he was making some bad decisions in the things he was purchasing," according to *Driving While Black*.

It's not hard to see why someone would question her reasoning. Does she normally worry about what customers are purchasing and call the police on them?

Also, the police could have handled the situation differently. Instead of immediately arresting the young man, they could have talked to him first. They could have questioned the clerk about the reason for her call. Those steps would have been better than being so quick to arrest an innocent man. The artist had to endure a humiliating situation for nothing.

Black shoppers can face discrimination from store employees, whether they make a purchase or not. Retailers may assume, incorrectly, that black shoppers steal more than others.

Because the clerk won't admit to racial profiling, you can't say with certainty that that's why she called the police. However, the reason she gave for the phone call isn't a very believable one, because it's not her job to decide that customers are making bad decisions.

What to Do if You're Stopped by the Police

You may have already been in a situation where you were racially profiled. You might have family and friends who have their own stories of discrimination. While it's understandable that you feel angry in these situations, the way you handle them can make a big difference.

No one wants to end up a police shooting statistic. More white people are shot and killed by police officers than black and brown people. But the percentages are disproportionate. According to an article in the *Washington Post*, in 2017, 46 percent of people fatally shot by police were white. Black victims made up 23 percent, and Hispanic victims made up 18 percent.

According to the US Census, Hispanics are about 18 percent of the total US population. So the percentage of Hispanic shooting victims is in line with their overall population in this country. This isn't the case with white and black victims. Whites make up about 60 percent of the US population,

the information right then. If not, remember as much as you can and write it down later. Record the date, the time, and the location where you were stopped. The more details you have about the incident, the better. These facts that will be helpful when you report the incident, and can be effective in getting you the assistance you need.

It can feel like a big hassle to have to follow an officer's orders when you feel like you're being harassed. You might say that other people of color followed orders and ended up being killed by the police anyway.

Just one example occurred in the summer of 2016, when police officer Jeronimo Yanez shot and killed Philando Castile in St. Paul, Minnesota. Yanez pulled over Castile's car for a broken taillight. Yanez asked Castile for his driver's license and registration. When Castile reached for them, Yanez shot him several times as Castile sat in his car. Castile's girlfriend and her young daughter were also in the car. His girlfriend recorded the aftermath of the shooting and aired it over social media.

This shooting happened very soon after the shooting death of Alton Sterling in Baton Rouge, Louisiana. In that case, police officers responded to a call to a convenience store. They heard there was a man there with a gun. Sterling was standing outside of the store. Officers arrested him and pinned him to the ground. That's when at least one of the officers shot him. Again, the incident was caught on cell phone video and quickly shown on television and social media channels.

Racial tensions skyrocketed after two shootings of unarmed black men so close together. What made tensions worse for people in the black community is the feeling that the victims never get justice. The police officers were never charged with any crimes, even though the evidence was recorded.

Remember, your first priority is survival. If you're alone in a situation like this, it's crucial to follow all orders. Without witnesses, there's no one to support your story if something bad happens.

Once safely at home, take steps to report any officers who abused their authority. You and your family may decide to contact an attorney, the media, or an organization like the ACLU.

How to Fight Racism and Racial Profiling

You don't have to fight against someone who's biased against you. This can be dangerous and lead to serious problems.

Instead, you can fight to make changes to how things currently are in society. Helping to make changes to laws and policies is a more positive step

Protests took place around the United States after two high-profile police shootings happened just days apart. Here protesters in New York make their voices heard.

to take. It can make you feel empowered when you know you're doing something to make a difference that helps so many others.

- **Vote**. One of the biggest things you can do, when you're old enough, is to vote. One of the reasons there's racial disparities in health care, schools, and living environments is because of who makes the laws. Some lawmakers don't

By voting, you can make a difference! You can work to elect officials who care about fighting discrimination at every level.

91

move to make positive changes for certain groups. They may pass laws that favor the wealthy over the poor. Some of these laws affect the length of time people go to jail for minor offenses. According to *Policing the Black Man* by Angela J. Davis, when it comes to drug offenses, black people go to jail more often and for longer periods of time than white people. When you exercise your right to vote, you help choose who holds important positions. You can work to elect politicians who promise to fight injustice.

- **Speak up whenever you see incidents of racism.** Record them on your phone if you can. Social media has exposed a lot of discriminatory practices and racist situations. By making these incidents public, people can see that racism exists. That can persuade them to take action against it, starting in their own communities.

- **Join others who are fighting against discrimination.** You might join a group that's involved in social activism. Together, you might decide to take part in peaceful protests.

When everyone works together, it's possible to make huge positive changes. By spreading knowledge and compassion for others, you contribute to a society where everyone is accepted for who they are.

Racism and racial profiling won't disappear overnight. But by making positive changes wherever you can, and encouraging others to embrace diversity and inclusion, you're working to make things better. In time, America could be a nation where the color of your skin never stands in your way, whether you're Asian, black, Hispanic, Latino, Native American, or white.

10 Great Questions to Ask a Social Activist

1. How can I stand up against discrimination when I see it happening to someone else?

2. How do I stand up against racism if I feel someone is discriminating against me?

3. What are my rights if I think I'm being discriminated against?

4. How can young people make a difference in their communities?

5. What should I do if a worker is following me around a store or treating me differently than he's treating other customers?

6. What are positive ways to protest against unfair policies?

7. What are some things I can do in my community to fight discrimination?

8. How do I stay safe when I'm speaking out against injustice?

9. What are the best ways to fight injustice?

10. What can I do if I'm surrounded by people who hold racist views and say racist things?

appeal A request to a higher court to reverse a decision.

dashcam A video camera that sits on a car's dashboard that constantly records the view outside of the windshield.

derogatory An attitude of treating people with little value.

detain To hold someone in custody, usually for questioning.

discrimination The unfair treatment of another person based on his or her race, gender, or age.

disproportionate Too big or too small compared to something else.

diversity A variety of different things.

harass To intimidate or pressure someone.

inclusion The act of including others in a group.

juvenile detention center A jail-like setting for minors.

lawsuit A claim brought to a court of law.

oppress To keep someone in a state of hardship.

penitentiary A prison for those who are convicted of serious crimes.

segregated Divided or separated, especially along racial lines.

snitch To tell on someone.

subtle Indirect and not obvious.

systematic Done according to a system or plan.

traffickers People who deal in illegal goods.

trespassing To be on a property without permission.

unconscious bias An attitude toward a person or group that someone may not be aware of.

violation The act of breaking a rule or law.

For More Information

American Civil Liberties Union (ACLU)
125 Broad Street, 18th Floor
New York NY 10004
(212) 549-2500
Website: https://www.aclu.org
Facebook and Twitter: @ACLU
The ACLU is an organization that works to
    defend and preserve American rights under
    the US Constitution.

Anti-Defamation League (ADL)
605 Third Avenue
New York, NY 10158-3560
(212) 885-7700
Website: https://www.adl.org
Facebook: @anti.defamation.league
Twitter: @ADL_national
Instagram: @adl_national
Email: adlmedia@adl.org
The ADL is an organization devoted to stopping
    discrimination against Jewish people. It promotes
    justice and fair treatment for everyone.

Asian Americans for Equality (AAFE)
807 48th Street
Brooklyn, NY 11220
(718) 686-8223
Website: https://www.aafe.org
Facebook and Twitter: @aafe1974
Instagram: @aafenyc
Email: askaafe@aafe.org
AAFE is an organization working to enrich the
    lives of Asian Americans. It promotes equal
    rights through social services and community
    development.

Canadian Centre for Diversity and Inclusion (CCDI)
Eastern Office:
820–2 Carlton Street
Toronto, ON M5B 1J3
Canada
(416) 968-6520
Western Office:
1805–500 4 Avenue SW
Calgary, AB T2P 2V6
Canada
(403) 879-1183
Website: https://ccdi.ca

Facebook: @CCDISOCIAL

Instagram: @ccdigrams

Twitter: @CCDITweets

CCDI is a Canadian organization that helps
employers and human resources professionals
address equity, diversity, and inclusion in the
workplace.

Council on American-Islamic Relations (CAIR)

453 New Jersey Avenue, SE

Washington, DC 20003

(202) 488-8787

Website: https://www.cair.com

Facebook and Twitter: @CAIRNational

Instagram: cair_national

Email: outreach@cair.com

The mission of CAIR is to promote understanding
of Islam. The organization also protects civil rights
and works to empower American Muslims.

Global Diversity Exchange (GDX)

Ryerson University

415 Yonge Street, Suite 701

Toronto, ON M5B 2E7

Canada

Website: http://www.globaldiversityexchange.ca
Facebook: @CitiesOfMigration
Twitter: @GDXryerson
Email: gdx@ryerson.ca
GDX is a Canadian organization working to help
    individuals, communities, and governments
    become immigrant-competent and immigrant-
    confident. GDX works for an international
    reach and uses academic and research methods.

National Coalition on School Diversity (NCSD)
c/o Poverty & Race Research Action Council
740 15th Street NW, 3rd floor
Washington, DC 20005
Website: http://school-diversity.org
Facebook: @diverse.schools
Twitter: @diverse_schools
Email: school-diversity@prrac.org
The NCSD is a network made up of research centers,
    civil rights organizations, and coalitions. The
    goal of the NCSD is expanding support for the
    promotion of diversity and integration.

Native American Rights Fund (NARF)
1506 Broadway

Boulder, CO 80302-6296

(303) 447-8760

Website: https://www.narf.org

Facebook: @NativeAmericanRightsFund

Twitter: @NDNrights

Email: infor@narf.org

NARF is an organization that provides legal
assistance to Native American individuals,
tribes, and organizations.

UnidosUS

1126 16th Street NW, Suite 600

Washington, DC 20036

(202) 785-1670

Website: https://www.unidosus.org

Facebook, Twitter, and Instagram: @
WeAreUnidosUS

Email: info@unidosus.org

UnidosUS advocates for the Hispanic community
through research and program work. The
organization serves Latinos in many areas,
including civil rights and immigration, health,
education, and housing.

For Further Reading

Abdel-Fattah, Randa. *The Lines We Cross*. New York, NY: Scholastic Press, 2017.

Behnke, Alison. *Racial Profiling: Everyday Inequality*. Minneapolis, MN: Twenty-First Century Books, 2017.

Delacre, Lulu. *Us, in Progress: Short Stories About Young Latinos*. New York, NY: HarperCollins, 2017.

Grinapol, Corinne. *Racial Profiling and Discrimination: Your Legal Rights*. New York, NY: Rosen Publishing, 2016.

Hanson-Harding, Alexandra. *I've Been Racially Profiled: Now What?* New York, NY: Rosen Publishing, 2015.

Merino, Noel. *Racial Profiling*. Farmington Hills, MI: Greenhaven Press, 2015.

Mooney, Carla. *Confronting Discrimination Against Immigrants*. New York, NY: Rosen Publishing, 2018.

Reynolds, Jason, and Brendan Kiely. *All American Boys*. St. Louis, MO: Turtleback Books, 2017.

Sanna, Ellyn. *Gallup Guide for Youth Facing Persistent Prejudice: Muslims*. Broomall, PA: Mason Crest Publishers, 2013.

American Civil Liberties Union. "School-to-Prison Pipeline," https://www.aclu.org/issues /juvenile-justice/school-prison-pipeline.

Bichell, Rae Ellen. "Scientists Start to Tease Out the Subtler Ways Racism Hurts Health." NPR, November 11, 2017. https://www.npr.org /sections/health-shots/2017/11/11/562623815 /scientists-start-to-tease-out-the-subtler-ways -racism-hurts-health.

Burnett, James H. III. "Racism Learned." *Boston Globe*, June 10, 2012. https://www .bostonglobe.com /business/2012/06/09/harvard-researcher -says-children-learn-racism-quickly /gWuN1ZG3M40WihER2kAfdK/story.html.

Davis, Angela J. *Policing the Black Man: Arrest, Prosecution, and Imprisonment*. New York, NY: Pantheon Books, 2017.

FBI. "2016 Crime in the United States," (2016): Table 21A, https://ucr.fbi.gov/crime-in-the -u.s/2016/crime-in-the-u.s.-2016/topic-pages /tables/table-21.

Fisher, Austin. "Wrongfully Detained Brothers Get ACLU Help." *Rio Grande Sun*, May 18, 2018.

http://www.riograndesun.com/news/city
/wrongfully-detained-brothers-get-aclu-help
/article_3093f18e-5adb-11e8-96a6
-e36df02710f7.html.

Flores, Antonio. "How the U.S. Hispanic Population
Is Changing." Pew Research Center, September 18,
2017. http://www.pewresearch.org/fact-tank
/2017/09/18/how-the-u-s-hispanic-population-is
-changing.

Harris, David A. *Profiles in Injustice: Why Racial
Profiling Cannot Work*. New York, NY: The New
Press, 2002.

Katz, Judy. *White Awareness: Handbook for Anti-
Racism Training*. Norman, OK: University of
Oklahoma Press, 1978.

Luongo, Michael T. "Traveling While Muslim
Complicates Air Travel." *New York Times*,
November 7, 2016. https://www.nytimes
.com/2016/11/08/business/traveling-while
-muslim-complicates-air-travel.html.

Makarechi, Kia. "What the Data Really Says About
the Police and Racial Bias," *Vanity Fair*, July 14,
2016. https://www.vanityfair.com
/news/2016/07/data-police-racial-bias.

Meeks, Kenneth. *Driving While Black: Highways, Shopping Malls, Taxicabs, Sidewalks: How to Fight Back if You Are a Victim of Racial Profiling.* New York, NY: Broadway Books, 2000.

Messenger, Tony, and Matt Sullivan. "I Could Have Been Mike Brown: Your Stories of Racial Profiling by the World's Police." *The Guardian,* August 29, 2014. https://www.theguardian.com /commentisfree/ng-interactive/2014/aug/29 /-sp-mike-brown-stories-racial-profiling-police.

Nielsen, Marianne O. and Robert A. Silverman, eds. "American Indians in Prison," *Native Americans, Crime, and Justice.* 1996, pp. 224-227. https://www.ncjrs.gov/App/Publications /abstract.aspx?ID=168158.

Quillian, Lincoln, Devah Pager, Arnfinn H. Midtboen, and Ole Hexel. "Hiring Discrimination Against Black Americans Hasn't Declined in 25 Years." *Harvard Business Review,* October 11, 2017. https://hbr.org/2017/10 /hiring-discrimination-against-black-americans -hasnt-declined-in-25-years.

Ross-Pilkington, Jack. "Mass Incarceration and Police Violence in Native American

Communities." Cornell Roosevelt Institute, November 3, 2017. https://www .cornellrooseveltinstitute.org/dom/mass -incarceration-and-police-violence-in-native -american-communities.

Salinas, Lupe S. and Fernando Colon-Navarro. "Racial Profiling as a Means of Thwarting the Alleged Latino Security Threat." *Race, Racism and the Law*, 2011. http://www.racism.org /index.php/articles/law-and-justice/criminal -justice-and-racism/130-racial-profiling /articles-related-to-racial-profiling/1502-latino -security-threat?showall=&start=2.

Sentencing Project, The. "Trends in U.S. Corrections," https://sentencingproject.org /wp-content/uploads/2016/01/Trends-in-US -Corrections.pdf.

Siegel, Rachel. "They Can't Be Here for Us: Black Men Arrested at Starbucks Tell Their Story for the First Time." *Washington Post*, April 19, 2018. https://www.washingtonpost.com/news /business/wp/2018/04/19/they-cant-be-here- for-us-black-men-arrested-at-starbucks-tell -their-story-for-the-first-time/?noredirect =on&utm_term=.c74b98c3ac7f.

Sourcebook of Criminal Justice Statistics Online, Table 3.106.2012.

Swaine, Jon, Oliver Laughland, and Jamiles Lartey. "Black Americans Killed by Police Analysis." *The Guardian*, June 1, 2015. https://www .theguardian.com/us-news/2015/jun/01/black -americans-killed-by-police-analysis.

Thomas, Angie. *The Hate U Give*. New York, NY: HarperCollins, 2017.

United States Sentencing Commission. "Demographic Differences in Sentencing: An Update to the 2012 Booker Report." November 2017: 2. https://www.ussc.gov /sites/default/files/pdf/research-and -publications/research -publications/2017/20171114_Demographics .pdf.

VanHook, Cortney R. "Racial Disparity in the Diagnosis of Conduct Disorder." (March 15, 2012): 8. https://scholarworks.gsu.edu/cgi /viewcontent.cgi?article=1038&context=univ _lib_ura.

Warikoo, Niraj. "Immigrants, Latinos in Michigan Say Border Patrol Agents Racially Profile," *Detroit Free Press*, May 17, 2018. https://www

.freep.com/story/news/2018/05/17/latinos
-michigan-immigration-agents-racially-profile
-buses-trains/575401002/.

Washington Post. "Fatal Force." https://www
.washingtonpost.com/graphics/national/police
-shootings-2017.

Yip, Tiffany, Gilbert C. Gee, and David T. Takeuchi.
"Racial Discrimination and Psychological
Distress: The Impact of Ethnic Identity and
Age Among Immigrant and United States-born
Asian Adults." *US National Library of Medicine,*
May 2008. https://www.ncbi.nlm.nih.gov/pmc
/articles/PMC2735246/.

About the Author

Del Sandeen is an author who is deeply interested in racial issues in the United States and abroad. As the daughter of an immigrant, she champions diversity and inclusion. She lives in Florida, which is just one state that has had high-profile cases involving racial profiling that led to racial tensions. Sandeen has written about the need for more diversity in publishing because she believes that representation matters. In addition to *Coping with Racial Profiling*, she has authored a biography on the relationship between President Thomas Jefferson and an enslaved woman, Sally Hemings.

Photo Credits

Cover Yuri Arcurs/E+/Getty Images; p. 5 Yuri Arcurs/E+/Getty Images; p. 6 Laura Buckman/AFP/Getty Images; p. 7 © AP Images; p. 11 Douglas Sacha/Moment Open/Getty Images; p. 12 living _images/E+/Getty Images; p. 15 SOPA Images/LightRocket/Getty Images; p. 18 New York Daily News Archive/Getty Images; p. 19 Stephanie Keith/Moment/Getty Images; p. 27 Rena Effendi/National Geographic/Getty Images; p. 29 William B. Plowman/Getty Images; p. 31 Doug Menuez/Photodisc/Getty Images; p. 32 asiseeit/E+ /Getty Images; p. 38 Ted Soqui/Corbis News/Getty Images; p. 44 Hero Images/Getty Images; p. 48 FatCamera/E+/Getty Images; p. 50 Guy Cali/Corbis/Getty Images; p. 58 Steve Debenport/E+ /Getty Images; p. 60 Haidar Hamdani/AFP/Getty Images; p. 63 NurPhoto/Getty Images; p. 67 Steve Osman/Los Angeles Times /Getty Images; p. 70 Image Source/Getty Images; p. 75 filadendron /E+/Getty Images; p. 78 alexsl/iStock Unreleased/Getty Images; p. 80 Hill Street Studios/Blend Images/Getty Images; p. 84 Bambu Productions/The Image Bank/Getty Images; p. 90 Yana Paskova /Getty Images; p. 91 adamkaz/E+/Getty Images.

Design and Layout: Nicole Russo-Duca; Editor: Elissa Petruzzi; Photo Researcher: Nicole Reinholdt